ILLUMINATE

A GUIDED ADVENT JOURNAL FOR PRAYER AND MEDITATION

FR. JOHN NEPIL

Ave Maria Press · AVE · Notre Dame, Indiana

Visit our website to find online components, including videos by Fr. John Nepil, to enhance your experience with *Illuminate* this Lent. Go to **www.avemariapress.com/pages/illuminate-resources**.

Scripture quotations are from the *Revised Standard Version of the Bible—Second Catholic Edition (Ignatius Edition)*, copyright © 2006 National Council of the Churches of Christ in the United States of America. Used by permission. All rights reserved.

Nihil Obstat: Reverend Monsignor Michael Heintz, PhD
  Censor Librorum
Imprimatur: Most Reverend Kevin C. Rhoades
  Bishop of Fort Wayne–South Bend
  Given at Fort Wayne, Indiana, on April 7, 2025

Founded in 1865, Ave Maria Press is a ministry of the United States Province of Holy Cross.

www.avemariapress.com

Paperback: ISBN-13 978-1-64680-423-8

E-book: ISBN-13 978-1-64680-424-5

Cover and interior images © Getty Images.

Cover and text design by Brianna Dombo.

Printed and bound in the United States of America.

WE ARE IN THE SEASON OF
ADVENT, AND IT SENDS A SHIVER
OF FEAR THROUGH US,
WARNING US OF THE APPROACH
OF SOMETHING THAT IS FINAL
AND ULTIMATE;
IT IS AS INEVITABLE AS THAT AN
EXPECTANT MOTHER MUST GIVE
BIRTH,
AS CERTAIN AS THAT A VOICE IN
THE WILDERNESS PRESUPPOSES
SOMEONE CRYING OUT.

HANS URS VON BALTHASAR,
YOU CROWN THE YEAR
WITH YOUR GOODNESS

CONTENTS

INTRODUCTION

THE COMING OF THE LIGHT

"Long winter nights make the stakes come alive." With these words, Bishop Erik Varden invites us into the mysterious northern reaches of his Norwegian diocese. There the sun has now set, not to reappear until the middle of January. For him, it is singularly meaningful to reflect on Christmas in light of the darkness of the northern hemisphere. For in those glaciated places, at the fringe of eternal snows, the darkness has set, revealing our fundamental need for interior illumination.

Advent is a journey into darkness. It is a liturgical reflection upon a planet's ever-so-gentle tilt away from the sun. The climactic moment, known as the winter solstice, is the celebration not simply of the presence of darkness but of the coming of the light. It was not a coincidence, nor pagan appropriation, that settled the festivity of Christmas on the short day of midwinter; it was the reality of the light, manifested fully and anew in the revelation of the God.

"This is the message we have heard from him and proclaim to you, that God is light and in him is no darkness at all" (1 Jn 1:5). This self-disclosure of God's inner life was made manifest in the words of Jesus Christ: "I have come as light into the world, that whoever believes in me may not remain in darkness" (Jn 12:46). Since the fourth century, the Church has professed this about Jesus: He is "God from God, light from light, true God from true God."

If we do not embrace the darkness, we cannot welcome the light. This is the heart of Advent: a season of trustful surrender, renewed receptivity, a silence in vigil. In this season, we are drawn again to the Marian hearth in the house of the Church to draw warmth and newness of strength. And it is the moment when we wait for the coming of the light—not just in the Christ-child at Christmas but in the inner illumination of God's presence in the soul. God, who is conceived in silence and born in poverty, comes again to fill the soul with light.

Our Advent meditations, centered on the theme of God as light, will step daily toward Christmas on a slow walk through the prologue of St. John (Jn 1:1–14). Our four-week path will tread four themes: Word, Light, Faith, and Life. Our guides will be Adrienne von Speyr and Hans Urs von Balthasar—the former a mystic, the latter her theological interpreter. Drawing from their inspiration, we will attempt to spiritually interpret the *chiaroscuro* of human life so as to find ourselves ready for the coming of the Child this Christmas.

For now, we bid farewell to the light. Let the stakes come alive.

HOW TO USE
THIS JOURNAL

The *Illuminate* Advent journal combines daily meditations, questions for reflection, journaling space, prayers, and beautiful original art to draw you into a deeper, richer experience of Advent. It helps prepare you not only to experience the magnitude of Jesus's birth but to contemplate the Incarnation of Christ in a personal way.

Over the next four weeks, we will take a slow walk through the prologue of St. John (Jn 1:1–14), which will sound familiar when you recall the first line: In the beginning was the Word. Line by line, we will contemplate the words and the meaning of the message St. John is striving to convey.

As we embark on this journey together, we have a unique opportunity set before us to *illuminate* the Word of God and to recognize the profundity of eternity entering human history. Through the meditations, prayers, scriptures, and insights from Swiss theologian Hans Urs von Balthasar found in this journal, you will be invited to slow down, reflect, prepare, and create space for daily encounters with God.

WHO IS *ILLUMINATE* FOR?

Illuminate is for anyone who desires to experience the Advent season as an opportunity to contemplate and anticipate the mystery of the Incarnation—the reality of light overcoming darkness. The season of Advent is the ideal time to step back from your life and evaluate where you stand with God, yourself, and others. This Advent journal provides a daily path of prayer and reflection to enter more deeply into the mystery of God.

Illuminate was designed for use in a group setting. There is something special about taking this Advent journey with a community, whether that community is your entire parish, a small group, or your family. Visit www.avemariapress.com/pages/illuminate-resources for more information about bulk

discounts, a leader's guide, help with organizing a small group, videos from Fr. John Nepil discussing the theme for each week of Advent, and other resources to help you make the most of your time together with *Illuminate*.

You can also use *Illuminate*'s meditations and journaling prompts on your own to help you draw near to God, hear his voice in new ways, and pour out your heart to him as you turn your attention daily to the power of God's love. You may find that, this Advent, you're in special need of regular quiet times of connection with God; *Illuminate* is an excellent way to help you find that space each day.

HOW IS *ILLUMINATE* ORGANIZED?

Illuminate is organized into four parts:

✦ In week 1, you'll explore the mystery of the Word as the beginning of everything.

✦ In week 2, you'll reflect on the light that Christ brings into the world and our choice to receive or refuse it.

✦ In week 3, you'll focus on the pure gift of faith that God freely gives.

✦ In week 4, you'll deeply explore what it means to be born of God into new life.

Within each week, you'll encounter a simple daily pattern made up of the following parts:

+ In order to focus your thoughts on the key idea from that day's meditation, each day opens with a *quotation* from Adrienne von Speyr or Hans Urs von Balthasar—the former a mystic, the latter her theological interpreter.

+ The *meditation* from Fr. John Nepil draws out the message from the lines of John 1 and real-life examples that help us. An important aspect of our Advent preparation for the Savior's coming is to journey into the darkness so that we can appreciate the light at Christmas

+ The *reflection questions* challenge you to ponder and journal in response to the meditation, helping you identify practical ways to live out the Advent season more fully.

+ Finally, after you've read and journaled, the closing *prayer* provides a starting point for your own requests and prayers of thanksgiving and praise to God.

HOW SHOULD I READ *ILLUMINATE*?

This Advent journal's daily format is flexible enough to accommodate any reader's preferences: If you're a morning person, you may want to start your day with *Illuminate*, completing the entire day's reading, reflection, journaling, and prayer first thing in the morning. Or you may prefer to end your day by using *Illuminate* to focus your attention on Christ as you begin to rest from the day's activities. You may even decide to read and pray as a family in the morning and journal individually in the evening. The key is finding what works for you, ensuring that you have time to read carefully, ponder deeply, write honestly, and connect intimately with the Lord in prayer. Whatever approach you choose (and whether you decide to experience *Illuminate* with a group or on your own), be sure to visit www.avemariapress.com/pages/illuminate-resources for extra resources to help you get the most out of this special Advent journey.

Visit our website to find online components, including videos by Fr. John Nepil, to enhance your experience with *Illuminate* this Lent. Go to **www. avemariapress.com/pages/illuminate-resources**.

FIRST WEEK
OF ADVENT

WORD

FIRST WEEK OF ADVENT

SUNDAY

BEGINNING IS THE FORM OF THE
CHRISTIAN LIFE.

ADRIENNE VON SPEYR,
THE WORD[1]

IN THE BEGINNING
WAS THE WORD

The opening line of a great story is unforgettable. For Dickens, "It was the best of times, it was the worst of times"; for Tolstoy, "Happy families are all alike; every unhappy family is unhappy in its own way"; or more simply for Melville, "Call me Ishmael." In all of them, we find ourselves within an unfolding plot, confounded by its characters, and given again that thrill which comes with a new beginning.

But this is not the case with the Gospel of St. John. "In the beginning was the Word" is not an entry into a plot; it is an immersion into a mystery. We are transported back to the first words ever uttered: "In the beginning was God" (Gn 1:1). It is now a fugue, whose music initiates us at the precipice of the ineffable—a new creation within creation. The first line of the Gospel is, then, not the opening line of a story but the opening of a new reality. In reading it, we have crossed a metaphysical Rubicon.

But there was, in fact, a beginning to creation and the story of the world. There was a moment before which there was nothing. Then the clock starts, creation is set in motion, and the movement of history has begun. But what was before the beginning of the world? That was always the unsearchable realm of the beyond. But now it can be known: The Word is the beginning. "As the beginning, God declares *that* he is. As the word, he declares *who* he is."[2] This is the first truth and the lasting paradox of creation: it is not its own beginning; its beginning is the Word.

Advent has begun. With it comes the joys and anxieties of our preparations for Christmas. But beneath these lies the real purpose of the season—*nunc coepi* ("now I begin"). Deep down our hearts desire the conversion of a new beginning and a fresh start. But this cannot be satisfied in the personal resolutions and chronological restarts of the new year. No, the true desire for the real beginning demands the mysterious immersion of my life into the origin of all reality. "Wisdom excels folly as light excels darkness" (Eccl 2:13). The Christian life arises out of wisdom and light: I am becoming; God alone is the beginning. To truly begin means to make him my beginning. And that alone makes for a great human story.

REFLECTION

1. What is one concrete way you can put God first, as "the beginning" of every day, hour, or moment?
2. When we make ourselves "the beginning" of our lives, we become anxious, and we forget we are loved. This, in turn, prevents us from effectively loving others. Who is one person that you can intentionally put before yourself today?

PRAY

CHRIST JESUS,
YOU ARE THE WORD MADE FLESH AND
THE SPLENDOR OF THE FATHER.
YOU ARE THE LIGHT OF THE WORLD
AND THE LIGHT OF MEN.
COME INTO THE DARKNESS OF MY
HEART THIS DAY
THAT I MAY BECOME ILLUMINED BY
THE PRESENCE OF YOUR WORD.
BE THE BEGINNING AND THE ENDING
OF ALL I DO, ALL I SAY, AND ALL I AM.
JESUS, BE THE AUTHOR OF MY LIFE.
GRANT THAT I MAY LOVE YOU ALWAYS,
AND THEN DO WITH ME
WHAT YOU WILL.
AMEN.

FIRST WEEK OF ADVENT

MONDAY

TRUE LOVE ALWAYS SPRINGS
MORE FROM THE VISION OF THE
BELOVED'S LOVE-WORTHINESS
THAN FROM ONE'S INNER
IMPULSE TO LOVE.

HANS URS VON BALTHASAR,
THE GRAIN OF WHEAT[3]

AND THE WORD WAS WITH GOD

Human life is conceived in the darkness of a mother's womb. Hidden in silence, a body quietly augments, informed and quickened as it is by an immaterial soul. From the dyadic rhythm of the maternal *lub-dub*, a single truth emerges—reality is *being-with*.

Then the child is born, at once blinded by the light. The separation is violent as the warmth of the womb is replaced by a precarious and cold world. The same holds true for conversion, like that of Paul in Damascus: "I could not see because of the brightness of that light" (Acts 22:11). We must be swaddled and drawn back to the heart of the mother. There the miracle happens: The child finds himself beheld in the gaze of the mother; and the Christian, in the gaze of our mother the Church. This is the founding event of human existence. The child comes to know that love exists, long before he will realize that he exists. These are the relational grounds of human life: that we come to self-consciousness only in and through the loving gaze of our mother.

In a mysterious way, the *being-with* of the mother and child images the inner life of the eternal God. As "the Word was with God" (Jn 1:1), *being-with* must be mysteriously contained within the life of God. This is the great secret of God's inner life: He is an eternal exchange of interpersonal love. Within human life, nothing images this so deeply as the way that the gaze of a mother envelops the entire subjectivity of the child. Perhaps God himself wanted to experience this, and thus he was "born of a woman" (Gal 4:4).

"Only when the beginning expresses itself as word are we able to learn to know God."[4] Our being is meant to radiate the light of God. But when our actions are not informed by the *being-with* logic of reality, we dim the light. If Advent is to be for us a coming of the light, it must first be a return to being.

Remember your mother: Long before she was *being-for*, she was simply *being-with*. These are not only the grounds of human life; they are the paradigm for Christian existence. So let us continue our return to the beginning, to the Word who is with God, so as to live according to the founding event of our life—*being-with*.

REFLECTION

1. Think of the lives of the saints. They were holy because even while on earth they were in a constant state of "being with" God by always being aware of his presence and by praying without ceasing (1 Thes 5:17). What is one way you can remind yourself of the silent presence of God throughout today?

2. By giving ourselves to God in silence, we allow him to create new things within our hearts. Where is a place in your life that you fill with unnecessary noise? How can prayerful silence be incorporated into that place today?

PRAY

MOTHER MARY,
LADY OF SWEETNESS AND
CONTEMPLATIVE BEAUTY,
BE WITH ME THROUGHOUT THIS DAY.
MAKE WITHIN MY HEART A PLACE OF
RECEPTIVE SILENCE,
JUST AS WAS IN YOUR HEART AT THE
MOMENT OF THE ANNUNCIATION
WHEN YOU RECEIVED JESUS
INTO YOURSELF.
THROUGH THIS SILENCE, LEAD US TO
THE HARMONIOUS BIRTH
OF YOUR SON,
THAT WE MAY RECEIVE HIM WITH
UTMOST PEACE AND JOY.
AMEN.

TUESDAY

ADORATION IS LOVE
OVERWHELMED BY THE BEAUTY,
THE POWER, THE IMMENSE
GRANDEUR OF THE LOVED.

HANS URS VON BALTHASAR,
THE GRAIN OF WHEAT[5]

AND THE WORD WAS GOD

A silent crowd was arrested as the symphony drew to a close. Gregory Alan Isakov, an acoustic musician and the evening guest, bowed his head in reverence as if seated in a garden of strings, brass, and percussion. The moment was still with the weight of eternity. We had beheld something and were enraptured. It was the most beautiful music we had ever heard.

The moment recalls Tolkien's vision of the creation. In his *Silmarillion*, Middle-earth comes to be through the music of the Ainur. The beauty of musical form expresses the meaningfulness of the Word. But it is communicated precisely as form, a perception that defies rational explanation. Unlike our reason, which often seeks to grasp and comprehend, the intuitive nature of perceived beauty does the opposite—we become its captives.

God "dwells in unapproachable light" (2 Cor 6:14) and is only known in and through the Word. And that Word is pre-existent and consubstantial with the Father. This is the mystery of Jesus Christ, true God from true God. He is the inner content, as well as the radiating form, of our every experience of truth, goodness, and beauty. Our task then is to adopt a posture of attunement to this mystery. Like the symphony we experienced that night, not only were the musicians attuned to one another, but we the captive audience found ourselves attuned to the beautiful. In that sense, it was an experience of God, of the Word-structure of reality that underlies the mystery of creation.

We are tempted to reduce the Christian life to "getting our act together." But if the essence of life in Christ is attunement, then we must transcend the self-reliance beneath this moralistic framework. We are invited to abandon our project of self-perfection, and perhaps for a time, even our measurable experience of God. But we are never lost in the meaningless cacophony of human events: If the Word is God, then God is the meaning of the world. In this way, we can have the confidence to let ourselves be formed. "Joy and suffering are the one indivisible form of this ceaselessly expanding life, which consists of being burst open, that is, of life unfolding in the beginning."[6] It is time to face squarely the totality of our lives, the joys and sufferings, as a new beginning of expectant hope. May our hearts be attuned and our lives symphonic.

REFLECTION

1. In a world full of noise and distraction, what is one way you can become attuned to God and his beauty today?
2. God can often speak to our hearts through holy music, art, and reading. How can you incorporate these things into your life so as to become more aware of God's beauty?

PRAY

GRACIOUS GOD,
YOU ARE THE CREATOR OF ALL THINGS.
INCREASE IN ME TODAY AN
ATTENTIVENESS TO YOUR BEAUTY IN
MY LIFE.
ALLOW YOUR GLORY TO SHINE
THROUGH THE MUNDANE
SO THAT MY LIFE MAY BECOME A
SYMPHONY OF LIGHT AND LOVE.
MAKE MY EAR ATTENTIVE TO YOUR
MELODIOUS VOICE,
THAT I MAY FOLLOW
YOUR HEAVENLY TUNE.
AMEN.

FIRST WEEK OF ADVENT

WEDNESDAY

WORD AND SILENCE POSSESS
THE SAME TRANSPARENCY IN THE
LORD, FOR HE IS NOT ONLY THE
FATHER'S WORD. HE SIGNIFIES
JUST AS MUCH THE FATHER'S
SILENCE.

ADRIENNE VON SPEYR,
LUMINA AND NEW LUMINA[7]

HE WAS IN THE
BEGINNING WITH GOD

My father is the silent type. He speaks only when necessary, and his words are thoughtful and clear. As a child it brought a calm steadiness to my life, a kind of assurance that things were safe. To put it in an image, my father's silence was a protective hedge around the garden of my young heart. Only in adolescence did it strike me as restrictive, an unassailable wall. Now as the years have passed and his silence has deepened, it has returned me to the safety of my childhood.

By listening to the word of the Son, we must come more deeply to the silence of the Father. For in God, silence is not the absence of words but its paternal atmosphere. And all of this is contained in Jesus, he who as the Word of the Father is likewise his silence. "No one knows the Father except the Son" (Mt 11:27). How impossible to comprehend such words. Just as this is the beginning, it is the form and content of our daily search for meaning. When God is silent we presume him unresponsive. But as the great saints and mystics attest, it is precisely the opposite. When the Word, Jesus Christ, is silent in our hearts, his receptive love takes the form of the Father's self-gift. But the rhythm of this mystery requires the surrender of all control. When we do so, we enter into the movement: "For those who sat in the region and shadow of death light has dawned" (Mt 4:16).

God's inner life is an ellipse of word and silence. They contain and mutually indwell one another. The Father is the virginal silence at the far reaches of divine self-giving. The Son is the fecundity of word, arising in the eternal act of self-reception. And the Spirit is the bond of love uniting gift and reception, word and silence. Only twice does the Father speak, and it is simply a confession of the Son, the Word made flesh. In this sense, "even silence is a form and an expression of the word."[8] May the light shine in the garden of the soul, our hearts hedged in the silence of the Father.

REFLECTION

1. Where are the places in your heart in which you try to prevent God from forming his protective hedge?
2. When we are constantly surrounded by noise, we can easily forget that God speaks to us; but silence helps us to recognize that voice. How will you make room for silence today?
3. The mystery of the Incarnation requires the surrender of all control. Which parts of your heart do you struggle to surrender to God?

_____

_____

_____

_____

_____

PRAY

*HEAVENLY FATHER,
YOU ARE THE DIVINE GARDENER,
YOU UPROOT ALL WHICH IS NOT TRUE,
AND YOU PROTECT ALL WHICH IS
GOOD WITHIN ME.
REVEAL TO ME THIS DAY
THE PLACES WHICH YOU STILL MUST
TEND TO.
I GIVE YOU FULL PERMISSION TO
UPROOT THE WEEDS
OF THE LIES IN MY HEART,
TO LET BLOSSOM THE FLOWERS OF
YOUR LOVE,
AND TO SILENTLY HEDGE IN THOSE
GIFTS WHICH YOU HAVE GRACIOUSLY
GIVEN ME.
ALL THIS FOR YOUR GREATER GLORY.
AMEN.*

FIRST WEEK OF ADVENT

THURSDAY

ALL CREATURES TELL, IN THEIR
OWN LANGUAGE, WHAT GOD IS
IN THEM

HANS URS VON BALTHASAR,
THE GRAIN OF WHEAT[9]

ALL THINGS WERE
MADE THROUGH HIM

While living in Rome, I once heard someone say *"Non c'é due senza tre."* I awkwardly translated it as "There is no two without three," which made no sense. It is idiomatic, with a meaning not deducible from its individual words. I later found out its translation: "Everything happens in threes."

What Italians intuit in the texture of human experience is revealed in what God has disclosed: The origin of all creation is trinitarian in form. Everything happens in threes because it was created by three. This three-ness of things, or trinitarian pattern, is disclosed in the Word, which is in the beginning with God. And then creation occurs, when "all things were made through him" (Jn 1:3). This happens not just through Jesus but truly within the space of trinitarian sonship. "In him all things were created" (Col 1:15).

Everything in creation speaks of God, everything revealed in the Word. It has a trinitarian form, an undeniable embossment. This stamp, impressed upon the being of things, becomes a watermark on the paper of human history. And thus, the things of our lives seem to happen in threes. For man, who stands at the pinnacle of creation with a capacity for God, this is not merely a carving—it is a mission: "Since man's created nature bears the seal and impress of the Trinity in its being, its spirit and its love, he can only understand himself and live rightly if he understands himself and lives through the Trinity."[10] The love of man and woman must open itself to the child if it is to truly live; and all human action must follow accordingly. Creation makes its return to God in the prayer of man, a resonance of trinitarian soundings. Through it we become "the light of the world"; and the Church, "a city on a hill" (Mt 5:14). But the subject must surrender the object and let things be in and through the Word. And come what may, let it be in threes.

REFLECTION

1. All of us are made in the image and likeness of God. What is one way that you can intentionally remind yourself of the dignity and beauty of each human person in your day-to-day life?
2. What is one way you can honor this dignity in another?
3. Do you see yourself as if you are made in the image and likeness of God? Do you speak to yourself and think of yourself as such? How does the Father speak to and see you?

PRAY

*BLESSED JESUS,
YOU SPRING FROM THE LOVE BETWEEN
THE FATHER AND THE SPIRIT,
TEACH ME TO HAVE
SUCH A LOVE FOR SOULS
THAT I CANNOT HELP BUT RECOGNIZE
YOUR FACE IN EACH ONE.
SHOW ME THE SWEET LOVE YOU HAVE
FOR ME, JESUS.
BRING ME INTO THE LOVING ARMS OF
THE FATHER.
LET ME BE SET AFLAME WITH THE FIRE
OF THE SPIRIT.
HELP ME TO SHARE THESE THINGS
THAT YOU REVEAL TO THE SOULS
AROUND ME.
JESUS, GIVE ME A GENEROUS SPIRIT,
THAT WHEN YOU ARE BORN TO US
AT CHRISTMAS,
I MAY KNOW MORE FULLY HOW TO
SHARE YOUR FRAGRANCE EVERYWHERE
I GO.
AMEN.*

FIRST WEEK OF ADVENT

FRIDAY

SELF EXISTS TOTALLY WITHIN
SELF-GIVING.

HANS URS VON BALTHASAR,
YOU HAVE WORDS OF ETERNAL LIFE[11]

AND WITHOUT HIM
WAS NOT ANYTHING MADE
THAT WAS MADE

It is Saturday, and one of our deacons is baking sourdough. It is an ancient practice that he takes up with the solemnity of a monastic rhythm. Patience, sensitivity, and attentiveness are the main ingredients along with flour, salt, and water. Its process is cyclical; first the cultivation of life, then the casting in the fires of death. In the end, it has become the new life of sustenance, nourishment for the human body.

"Without him nothing" (Jn 1:3). Here we must reverentially pause to reflect on the real state of creation. Beneath the modern fallacy of a self-sustaining world is the reality that without God there is nothing. Perhaps the Word is the yeast of creation, leavening throughout centuries for the arrival of the bread of life.

If only it were that simple, if only he were received. "Beware of the leaven of the Pharisees" (Mt. 16:6), he tells us. Beware of the yeast of self-reliance, constructions of self-perfection and religious technology, veiling the will to power. Beware of thinking anything has been made apart from him.

His response was the glorious institution of the Eucharist. This bread from heaven is not merely a sign of his crucified body; it is a sharing in his eternal self-surrender to the Father. The self cannot find itself apart from his selflessness. "It is only in the word that man awakens to himself."[12]

If we are to become the living bread of Christ for the nourishment of the world, then we must be configured to his self-giving love. Our lives must become entirely Eucharistic, wholly surrendered so as to be totally given. The poor we always have with us, and they stand in need of a Church that can feed them with the bread of Eucharistic love. But it all hinges on that first and fundamental truth, that without him nothing has been made. Once this truth begins to grow in us, we stand ready to be kindled. "Walk by the light of your fire" (Is 50:11).

REFLECTION

1. Name the places in your life where you place false hope or security, "the leaven of the Pharisees." How can you let Jesus into those places so that you may learn to fully trust in him?
2. Jesus cannot come into a house that is already full of something else. In order to prepare a place for the bread of Eucharistic love within you, what can you give up in sacrifice this Advent?
3. How would your life change if you lived fully acknowledging that without him nothing has been made?

_____

_____

_____

_____

_____

_____

_____

_____

_____

PRAY

GOOD JESUS,
YOU ARE THE ONE TO WHOM ALL
GOOD THINGS RISE.
BE THE LEAVEN IN MY HEART THIS DAY.
TEACH ME TO ASCEND TO YOUR HOLY
LOVE EVEN WHILE I AM ON THE EARTH,
SO THAT, WHEN YOU DEEM THE
RIGHTFUL HOUR,
I MAY BECOME TOTALLY SET ABLAZE
WITH HOLY LOVE FOR YOU.
AMEN.

FIRST WEEK OF ADVENT

SATURDAY

THE MORE MYSTERIOUS GOD
IS TO YOU, THE CLOSER HE IS
TO YOU.

ADRIENNE VON SPEYR,
LUMINA AND NEW LUMINA[13]

IN HIM WAS LIFE

I met Matilda four months too early. She was born premature. I baptized my goddaughter in an incubator, the size of a large shoebox, filled with a complex array of medical devices to keep her alive. As I looked down upon this tiniest of humans, there was a moment when I felt I could see her soul. That this was not just a random collection of animated matter but a small body revealing a person. This person was fighting for her life. But more importantly, she was alive.

When Jesus pronounced himself "the life" (Jn 11:25), he shattered all religious sensibility. The identification of life with God was conceivable, but life with a concrete man in the flesh, implausible. But the fact remains: He alone is the revelation of the Father, access to "the fountain of life" (Ps. 36:8). God does not have life; he is life. And all life is his impartation.

Human life is destined for death. In this sense, it is more than a problem—it is a tragedy. The basic grounds of the Christian claim are the conquest of life over death, accomplished by life itself. From this angle one sees that the old life has died in Christ and that a new life has begun. Grace imparts a divine life, one that deifies and draws into an unfathomable union.

The depth of intimacy between God and man lies in the gift of life. But this life is also the Word, which means that the shape of life is itself a movement into meaning. Christ unites the three-fold cord of the way, truth, and life into his divine personhood, which is the Word. Bound by this cord, we begin to interpret our experience within the meaningfulness of love. "It is only when we give all that is incomprehensible in our lives back to the clear unity of God's life that we can live and our life ceases to be a problem."[14] Matilda doesn't know this, nor does she need to. "If your eye is sound, your whole body will be full of light" (Mt 6:22). In the miracle of her soul lies the mystery of light, word, and love.

REFLECTION

1. Do you treat your own life and the lives of others as a gift from God? If so, why? If not, what needs to change?
2. What are some ways God has shown you his love in recent days? Thank him daily for these graces.

_____

_____

_____

_____

_____

_____

_____

_____

PRAY

HEAVENLY FATHER,
FROM YOU ALL BLESSINGS FLOW,
FROM YOU ALL CREATED THINGS
RECEIVE THE GIFT OF LIFE.
PENETRATE MY LIFE SO THAT YOUR
RAYS ARE MADE VISIBLE TO ALL
WILLING TO BEHOLD.
ENVELOP MY HEART IN YOUR LIGHT,
THAT I MAY BECOME UNRECOGNIZABLE.
MAKE OF MY LIFE AN EXAMPLE OF
YOUR LOVE.
AMEN.

SECOND WEEK OF ADVENT

LIGHT

SECOND WEEK OF ADVENT

SUNDAY

DARE TO MAKE THE LEAP INTO
THE LIGHT! . . . MY KINGDOM
GROWS IN ALL OF YOU.

HANS URS VON BALTHASAR,
HEART OF THE WORLD[1]

AND THE LIFE WAS
THE LIGHT OF MEN

Alpenglow. Photographers call it "the magic hour." It is not first light, but the moment when light penetrates the mountains, bursting them into flame. Witnessing this from the heights gives a sense of the glory of battle. Twice a day we behold this optical phenomenon, once before sunrise and again after sunset. This reflected light is never static and flat but dynamically transformative. Alpenglow is light exploding into color upon the glory of the mountainside.

"God is light and in him is no darkness" (1 Jn 1:5). God, in himself, is the totality of light just as he is the fullness of life. The absence of darkness in God reveals the eternal simplicity of love, from which the Word was begotten. In him alone do life and light mutually indwell and co-penetrate.

But God cannot be known in himself, only in and through creation. Here, life and light must be distinguished. In the beginning, God said, "Let there be light" (Gn 1:3). Only afterward does he bring forth life in vegetative, sentient, and rational form. The new beginning is given to us in reverse; he comes as life, and that "life is the light of men" (Jn 1:4). Forever thereafter, "he who follows me will not walk in darkness, but will have the light of life" (Jn 8:12).

"Life and light are not absolutely the same. Life means giving and surrender; light is participation. Life unfolds, expands and spreads; light takes possession of the space thus created."[2] Jesus Christ, the word who is "a lamp for our feet and a light for our path" (Ps 119:105), must first restore life to a dead world before he can become the pure radiance of light. This is the paradox of the kingdom, which he, in time, will announce and consummate. But for now, in those minutes before dawn, we must attentively receive the light as God breaks forth upon a dark world in the splendor of alpenglow.

REFLECTION

1. In the past, how have you allowed Christ's light to transform you? How will you allow this same light to transform you in the future?
2. What is one concrete act of surrender you can make to the Lord today?
3. Look for an opportunity to do something for another today. How will you allow this moment of intentional charity to make Christ's light more visible to that person?

PRAY

GLORIOUS FATHER,
YOU SHAPED THE MOUNTAINS WITH
YOUR MIGHTY HAND
AND CAST ON THEM
YOUR HEAVENLY GLOW.
DO THE SAME TO MY SOUL THIS DAY.
COME INTO YOUR CREATION AND MAKE
IT SHINE IN AN ETERNAL ALPENGLOW.
ALLOW MY SOUL TO MAGNIFY YOUR
GREATNESS AND REJOICE IN YOU
COME CHRISTMAS.
AMEN.

SECOND WEEK OF ADVENT

MONDAY

THE NIGHT IS THERE TO REMIND
YOU OF YOUR POWERLESSNESS;
BLESS THE DARKNESS, FOR IT
SHOWS YOU THE LORD.

ADRIENNE VON SPEYR,
LUMINA AND NEW LUMINA[3]

THE LIGHT SHINES
IN THE DARKNESS

Much of humanity sleeps for a third of life. This fact stupefies the man of science, tailored in his evolutionary straightjacket. All living creatures, in some form, sleep. And strangely, all mammals dream. If we deprive ourselves of sleep, the physiological consequences are astounding. It is simply an absolute mandate of being human, one which, though tested, cannot be overcome. Daily the light passes to darkness, and we are forced to surrender ourselves to its irresistible power.

Night was created by God for us to sleep. We must remember this before we set off moralizing the darkness. God only creates out of his goodness; and thus the light he creates—as well as the darkness—is good. "The darkness he called night" (Gn 1:5). Though there is no darkness in God, the great poets of the Church, from the mystic John of the Cross to the contemporary Sally Read, have intuited that the created darkness of night reveals something of the primordial light of God. We can affirm that "light shines in the darkness" (Jn 1:5); but we cannot forget the night. "Even the darkness is not dark to thee, the night is bright as the day; for darkness is as light with thee" (Ps 139:12).

"There are three kinds of night: the night created by God, the quality of God that led him to create night and finally the night of sin created by man."[4] The first reveals the second in creation just as the third reveals it in the redemption. The stage upon which Jesus Christ is to act is the light shining in the darkness of sin. But when we collapse God's dark night into man's dark sin, we lose the inner meaning of the Cross. If our love is to be made cruciform, then we must discover in the dark night of love the hidden radiance of God's blinding light. Though "children of the light" (1 Thes 5:5), we remain confounded by darkness. Our path forward is the poetic repose of contemplation—that is, to sleep in God.

REFLECTION

1. How have you allowed a period of darkness in your life to form you in a positive way?
2. From where or whom do you find your rest?
3. What does "sleeping in God" look like for you in your daily life?

_____

_____

_____

_____

_____

_____

PRAY

BELOVED JESUS,
YOU ARE THE LIGHT IN THE DARKNESS.
MAKE ME A CHILD OF YOUR LIGHT
THIS DAY.
UPROOT ME FROM THE DARKNESS OF
THE WORLD,
AND SET ME ABLAZE WITH THE FIRE OF
YOUR SPIRIT.
BE MY LIGHT, BE MY REST,
BE MY SURETY.
YOU ARE MY ROCK, MY STRONGHOLD,
MY GOD IN WHOM I TRUST.
DO NOT EVER LET ME ESCAPE FROM
YOUR JOYFUL RAYS
OF LOVE AND PEACE.
AMEN.

SECOND WEEK OF ADVENT

TUESDAY

HE WAS THE LIGHT,

AND ALL WERE BLIND.

HANS URS VON BALTHASAR,
HEART OF THE WORLD[5]

AND THE DARKNESS
HAS NOT OVERCOME IT

"Midway upon the journey of our life / I found myself within a forest dark, / For the straightforward pathway had been lost." With these words Dante begins his odyssean journey of the *Inferno*. The forest dark, or *selva oscura* in the Italian, is the darkness of sin and the inescapable region of death. Dante wrote these words in 1308, several years after his exile from Florence. But he places himself in the story in the year 1300, the time when he was at the height of political prominence, wealth, and prestige. The darkness from which he seeks release is not the poverty of exile; it is the riches of the world (cf. 1 Tm 6:17).

The light of Christ has shown in the world, and "the darkness has not overcome it" (Jn 1:4). Another translation from the Greek is that the darkness "has not received it." This reveals the deeper, more insidious nature of sin; it is defiance, obstinance, refusal. But just like physical light overcoming darkness, the folly of sin's dark struggle is the delusion of the promethean. "For what fellowship has light with darkness?" (2 Cor 6:14).

What then is the essence of sin? It is "not enduring the dark night of love, of wanting to throw light on the darkness of God."[6] Sin is the refusal to endure the mystery. Man is unassailably blind. Because of this we cannot endure the light. But the reality of saving grace makes possible the experience of communion with God, "to walk in the light, as he is in the light" (1 Jn 1:6). We have been found, lost in the dark forest of our sins. To walk now in Christ means surrendering our path and enduring the dark mystery of God's love. It may lead to the experience of hell or perhaps the mount of Purgatory. But in the end, like Dante, we will look up at the darkness of night and behold the stars.

REFLECTION

1. Becoming too attached to the things of the world can cloud our ability to hear God's word. What material thing can you give away today so that you may draw nearer to the heart of the Father?

2. Walking by faith often means feeling lost and in the dark, but this is not actually the case. Where in your life do you need to beg God for the grace to walk by the light of faith?

PRAY

GOOD JESUS,
YOU ARE THE GOOD SHEPHERD.
YOU HAVE NEVER LET ONE OF
YOUR SHEEP BECOME LOST
IN THE WILDERNESS.
REASSURE ME OF THIS LOVE YOU HAVE
FOR ME TODAY.
SHOW ME THAT I HAVE NOT BEEN LOST.
BRING ME AGAIN
TO THE JOY OF THE NATIVITY.
REMIND ME AGAIN THAT AS LONG AS I
WALK BY THE VISIBLE LIGHT
OF YOUR GRACE,
AND NOT BY MY OWN FAULTY EYES,
YOU WILL NEVER LEAVE ME ALONE.
AMEN.

43

SECOND WEEK OF ADVENT

WEDNESDAY

SOMETIMES GOD SHOWS HIS
CLOSENESS PRECISELY BY
UNCOVERING THE DISTANCE.

ADRIENNE VON SPEYR,
LUMINA AND NEW LUMINA[7]

THERE WAS A MAN
SENT FROM GOD

In the ancient world, the stars were navigation. Everywhere they shone with a brilliance inconceivable to we moderns. No artificial light dimmed their radiance, no city kept them at bay. They were guiding principles, at once instructive and luminous, that offered humanity its path through the darkness of life. For this reason, they were known not as space but as the heavens.

To be human means to be with others. When God became man, he acknowledged his own creative logic. Jesus is born into relation with others, what could be called a Christological constellation. He, the "Daystar" (2 Pt 1:19), desires always to be known in and through his relations with others. And for that reason, another man "is sent by God" (Jn 1:6). He will be the first to behold the lamb of God (cf. Jn 1:23), revealing to creation that "the glory of God is its light, and its lamp is the Lamb" (Rv 21:23).

Even before we hear his name, we know his purpose: "The beginning and origin of his action is a mission: he is sent from God."[8] Mission is not something he does; it is something that he is. And within that mission, the dynamic interplay between God's closeness and nearness will be initiated with dramatic effect. But in order for him to be sent, he must receive a mandate of *noncomprehension*, a "not knowing" of what will come to pass. Something deeper than knowledge must guide him. Furthermore, identification with mission promises no control and demands total surrender. In this is revealed the true nature of life and love—and with it the end of our quest to possess love as a kind of proximate identity. No, the essence of love is a delicate dance of nearness and distance. John must live this before Jesus can impart it. As the last of the prophets, it is his sole task. He will be sent to the desert, into the dark wilderness of the world.

He does so to become the first star in the Christological constellation, which in time will become the Church.

REFLECTION

1. To be human means to be with others. How can you lend your time, a listening ear, a helping hand, etc. to a community or specific person near you?
2. We, like John, are led into a sort of desert (Advent) before Christ's coming at Christmas. Like John, how will you share the joy of the Gospel at Christmas?

PRAY

*MOTHER MARY,
YOU ARE THE MORNING STAR SO
STRONG AND BRIGHT.
WE CANNOT UTTER YOUR NAME
WITHOUT THE NAME OF YOUR SON
ECHOING IN RESPONSE.
POINT OUT TO US, STELLA MARIS, THE
WAY OF YOUR SON.
LEAD US ALWAYS INTO HIS PRESENCE.
PREPARE IN ME AN OASIS FOR CHRIST'S
BODY IN THE EUCHARIST.
PREPARE ME FOR CHRISTMAS; MAKE OF
ME A THING BEAUTIFUL FOR YOUR SON
TO BEHOLD.
AMEN.*

THURSDAY

IT IS NOT THEY WHO POSSESS
A MISSION, BUT THEIR MISSION
POSSESSES THEM.

HANS URS VON BALTHASAR,
YOU CROWN THE YEAR
WITH YOUR GOODNESS[9]

WHOSE NAME WAS JOHN

I retreat each year to the mountains for the summer solstice—the longest day of the year. We live in a tilted world of times and seasons, and now it is filled with light. On that longest and brightest of days, creation offers a liturgy of John the Baptist. The ancient practice of dating Christmas to December 25 comes from the even more ancient dating of the Feast of the Annunciation on March 25. Though not directly aligning to the summer and winter solstice, it is a fitting correspondence: "He must increase and I must decrease" (Jn 3:30).

The Old Covenant was held in twilight. Soft the light glows, refracted and strained, but never prevailing. We lived in this half light for millennia. Despite the luminosity of patriarchs, prophets, and great kings, there was never more than a fading light, one always receding into darkness. It was a kind of epochal advent: "In the sense of advent the Old Covenant inclines toward the New, and in the twilight appeared the man who was to bear witness to the light."[10]

In order to prepare the way for Christ, John must abide the dimness of this waning world. He will do so not merely by taking on his mission but by being entirely possessed by it. This will climax in the waters of repentance and culminate in the blood of martyrdom. His is a story of total dispossession. And Christ will affirm its significance: "Truly, I say to you, among those born of women there has risen no one greater than John the Baptist" (Mt 11:11). Herein lies the pattern of Christian existence. It starts in grace, which always implies a mission. But mission demands surrender. "Whoever loses his life for my sake will find it" (Mt 16:25). It is the inescapable path of his every disciple. The light will not and cannot come into the world unless we do as John did. The summer equinox is here, "darkness is passing away and the true light is already shining" (1 Jn 2:8).

REFLECTION

1. Bringing the light of Christ into the world requires that we be in the world though not of it. Which of the saints comes to mind when you think of this? Read about the life of that saint today, and imitate their example in your own life.
2. How do you feel God is calling you to mission this Advent?

_____

_____

_____

_____

_____

_____

_____

PRAY

FATHER IN HEAVEN,
BEFORE YOU FORMED ME IN THE
WOMB, YOU KNEW ME.
YOU KNOW THE FULLNESS
OF THE MISSION
TO WHICH I HAVE BEEN ASSIGNED.
GUIDE ME BY YOUR HOLY SPIRIT.
HELP TO MAKE STRAIGHT THE WAY OF
THE LORD.
SHINE YOUR LIGHT ON MY PATH,
THAT OTHERS MAY BE LED FROM THIS
EARTH TO YOUR PARADISE.
AMEN.

SECOND WEEK OF ADVENT

FRIDAY

CONVERSION IS ALWAYS A
PAINFUL AND LONELY PROCESS.

HANS URS VON BALTHASAR,
*YOU CROWN THE YEAR
WITH YOUR GOODNESS*[11]

HE CAME FOR TESTIMONY

I biked toward Big Sur, cliffs rising in defiance of the Pacific shore. It was a place of tumultuous beauty, an everlasting battlefield at the interstices of land and sea. And it speaks of human life: the waves of our dreams continually crashing upon the rocks of reality. All that remains is the spray—hope springing eternal.

When John appears on the world stage, his message is one of conversion. It is the Greek word *metanoia,* literally a "turning of the mind" away from the pilgrim world and back to our fatherland in God (cf. Rom 12:2). The Baptist "came for testimony" (Jn 1:7) and called us to conversion. We must convert so that we may give testimony.

The picture has already been framed: John is the voice; Christ, the Word. This insight of St. Augustine reveals the inner dynamic of Christian existence. A voice without a word is meaningless; a word without a voice, speechless. Language, as meaningful speech, is the union of the two in the enfleshed moment. It is the singular gift of the Holy Spirit that we could ever attain to such a thing. But it requires much labor on our end: a daily self-emptying of all preconceptions and judgments and any other attempts at control. Most of all, we must empty ourselves of desire to be the word—to be the center, source, and criteria of my life's meaning. In so emptying ourselves, we become his voice.

I cannot become the voice of the word except through relationships with others. "For knowledge of my neighbor may become the medium and mirror of self-knowledge and self-love. God has therefore made the Thou in his own image; everything in it is an image and symbol of what I know absolutely of God in faith."[12] Because of its "thou" structure, Christian faith is principally incarnational, not spiritual. The spiritualization of faith is deadly precisely because it eclipses God in the other. In every relationship (yes, even with our enemies), much is given, and much is expected (cf. Lk 12:48). Intrepid in love, let our "light so shine before men . . . and give glory to the Father" (Mt 5:16). This confidence of faith, despite knowing where things will end, frees us to ride the waves of providence.

REFLECTION

1. Do you notice a difference in your relationships with others when you use your words intentionally rather than to fill silence?

2. How may you be called to give testimony to God's goodness in your life? How could you do so on a daily business, whether in private gratitude or in public acknowledgment?

_____

_____

_____

_____

_____

_____

PRAY

LOVING JESUS,
YOU ARE ETERNAL WORD
AND ETERNAL MAN.
SPEAK INTO MY HEART AND THE
HEARTS OF ALL I ENCOUNTER,
THE TRUTH OF YOUR LOVE
AND YOUR GRACE.
YOU ARE THE LIGHT OF THE WORLD.
A CITY SET ON A HILL
CANNOT BE HIDDEN.
GIVE ME THE COURAGE AND THE
STRENGTH TO PROCLAIM YOUR
COMING TO THE NATIONS.
AMEN.

SECOND WEEK OF ADVENT

SATURDAY

THOSE WHO ENTER MY LIFE
SHOULD CATCH SIGHT NEITHER
OF ME NOR OF THE WAY I HAVE
UTILIZED THE LIGHT;
RATHER, THEY SHOULD SEE THE
LIGHT ITSELF.

HANS URS VON BALTHASAR,
YOU HAVE WORDS OF ETERNAL LIFE[13]

TO BEAR WITNESS
TO THE LIGHT

"God is my copilot." Though the intention of this bumper sticker is good, it entirely misses the point. We must ruthlessly eliminate every semblance of self-serving if we are to attain to the light. Our own light is not the clarifying tributary through which we canoe the waters of life. All that matters, all that is light, is his light. "In your light do we see light" (Ps 36:9). Time for us to exit the driver's seat.

"The first exceptional witness to the light of Christ was John the Baptist. He is the criterion and image of every subsequent form of testimony and mission."[14] The testimony born by John is the prophetic word needed to wake us from the slumber of our self-reliance. He fulfills the vision of the Old Covenant, which predicted that the light of God would come with such immensity that even the sun would not compare. "The sun shall be no more your light by day, nor for brightness shall the moon give light to you by night; but the Lord will be your everlasting light, and your God will be your glory" (Is 60:19).

In the witness of John to the light, the eyes of the world begin to open. But he had to traverse the darkness in order to bear this witness. We enjoyed him for a while (cf. Jn 5:35)—that is, until the testimony bore against our own light, our privatized sense of navigation. Though his testimony culminates in martyrdom, his words are interiorized in the teaching of Christ: "He who does what is true comes to the light, that it may be clearly seen that his deeds have been wrought in God" (Jn 3:21). Life in the light is a doing of the truth. God is not the copilot, nor a pilot at all. Life is not a machine to be driven; it is a mystery to behold. He remains "the God of the living" (Mk 12:27), calling us in faith to the unattainable heights of the Father.

REFLECTION

1. What is one practical way you can practice surrendering your life to God, making him not your copilot but your guiding light through the mystery of life?
2. How might someone "bear witness to the light" in their daily life like John the Baptist?

PRAY

HEAVENLY FATHER,
YOU ARE THE PERFECT LIGHT OF LOVE.
COME INTO MY HEART TODAY,
THAT THROUGH ALL THE CRACKS OF
BROKENNESS WITHIN ME,
YOU MAY SHINE FOR ALL THE WORLD
TO SEE.
BY MY IMPERFECTION,
MAKE ME A VESSEL FOR OTHERS TO
KNOW YOUR PERFECTION.
AMEN.

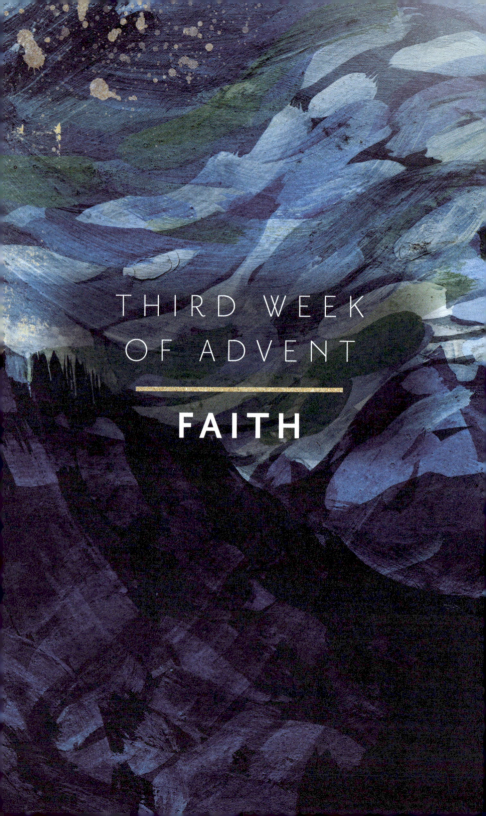

THIRD WEEK
OF ADVENT

FAITH

THIRD WEEK OF ADVENT

SUNDAY

CHRISTIANITY ALONE HAS GIVEN
MANKIND A TOTAL BLUEPRINT.

HANS URS VON BALTHASAR,
*YOU CROWN THE YEAR
WITH YOUR GOODNESS*[1]

THAT ALL MIGHT
BELIEVE THROUGH HIM

I left the retreat for reasons I couldn't understand. I was seventeen, faithless, and lost. And it was then that the priest left the ninety-nine and came after me. It felt like we talked for hours, but it may have been only a few minutes. It was too late before I realized I was hooked. I fought nonetheless and swam away downstream. At last, my strength was depleted, and I was brought into the barque of Christ with a twitch upon a thread.

"Everything is created through faith; it is the life and the light of man."[2] Faith is as illusive and indescribable as catching trout. It is pure gift. We look deeply into the dark waters of existence and see only a murky reflection of ourselves. Then the fly takes, the hook sets, and we feel the life of this mysterious creature beneath the surface of things. No wonder Christ called fishermen.

But faith is more than the personal experience of being found, caught, or rescued by Christ; it is about the salvation of the world. The fact that God "desires all men to be saved and to come to the knowledge of the truth" (1 Tm 2:4) is scandalously astonishing. Likewise for John, who gave testimony that all might believe through Jesus, the light (cf. Jn 1:7). The blueprint of faith has a social fabric, always concrete and ever relational. The Church is the place where Christ makes individuals into persons.

During the twentieth century, the world asked the Church, "What do you have to say for yourself?" The Church responded: *Lumen Gentium sit Christus*—Christ is the light of the nations. The Church never points to herself but, like John, can only gesture toward he who fulfills the old promise: "I am the Lord, I have called you in righteousness, I have taken you by the hand and kept you; I have given you as a covenant to the people, a light to the nations" (Is 42:6). Swim we may in the downstream current of history; but beware, he has made them "fishers of men" (Mt 4:19).

REFLECTION

1. Have you walked with the Lord your whole life? If yes, thank God for his tremendous grace. If no, what or who brought you back? Thank the Lord for his providence and fatherly love.
2. How will you use the God-given gift of your faith for the salvation of the world?
3. How can you use the gifts God has given you to deeply glorify him?

_____

_____

_____

_____

_____

_____

_____

_____

PRAY

HOLY SPIRIT,
YOU ARE THE GREATEST GIFT-GIVER.
THOUGH I DO NOT DESIRE YOU
BECAUSE OF YOUR GIFTS,
I NOW PRAISE YOU FOR THEM.
SHOW ME HOW I CAN USE THE GIFT OF
MY FAITH FOR THE GOOD OF OTHERS.
HELP ME TO USE ALL MY TALENTS FOR
THE GREATER GLORY OF GOD.
AMEN.

THIRD WEEK OF ADVENT

MONDAY

DISTANCE AS NEARNESS . . . A
PERSON WHO IS CONSCIOUS
OF THIS CAN BE A WITNESS
FOR GOD'S LIGHT WHILE
STEADFASTLY DENYING THAT HE
HIMSELF IS THE LIGHT.

HANS URS VON BALTHASAR,
LIGHT OF THE WORD[3]

HE WAS NOT THE LIGHT

I climbed my first mountain in fifth grade. It taught me more about what I was not than what I was. And I have endlessly craved that experience ever since. Transcendence can never be fabricated in our cities of concrete and glass. We have to go into the wild places, being totally immersed in the immensity of creation. We must breathe cold air under the pure sight of an infinite horizon. I become human again in the discovery of what I am not.

The lesson of the mountains calls for the virtue of hope. "He gives him hope to help him endure not being God. To exist in a state of dependence."[4] Hope is the perspectival virtue. It renders us capable of a life of creaturely tension: that I am contingent, dependent, and utterly reliant. Moreover, life is filled with false summits, when expectations collapse in anticipation. This bears the fruit of disenchantment, the shattering realization that I have yet to arrive. But from all this ash heap of experience is born something new—the fire of hope. Perspective is regained, a promise re-given. We are reborn in the discovery of the living God, he who abides in infinite distance and absolute nearness. A Christ-form radiates from creation, impressed upon our souls for its own testimony.

Set free from slavery, Israel was sustained through the wilderness by the hope of the Promised Land. God was present to them "in a pillar of fire to give them light, that they might travel by day and by night" (Ex 13:21). Beneath the numinous experience of theophany, the light of God created their path. He did so in distance and nearness, always as "a consuming fire" (Heb 12:29). What he taught his people he teaches us today: You are not the light of your path, nor the fire of your love. But from it you will always see and be warm. This is the source of our hope, our strength to climb mountains.

REFLECTION

1. What is one experience in your life where you became acutely aware of the presence of God? What brought you to that moment?

2. God wants you to be on fire for him whether you feel like you are or not. Have you let the inspiration from moments where you feel close to God come to a plateau when the feelings faded? How can you remain dependent on God even when you don't feel like it?

PRAY

*FATHER IN HEAVEN,
YOU CARE FOR
THE LILIES AND SPARROWS.
"DO YOU NOT MATTER MORE THAN
THESE?" YOU ASK.
REMIND ME OF THE CONSTANT
ATTENTION AND CARE YOU GIVE ME.
HELP ME TO BE AT PEACE, FULLY
SURRENDERING TO YOU AT ALL TIMES.
LEAD ME UP THE MOUNTAIN OF YOUR
LOVE SO THAT AT CHRISTMAS
I CAN CELEBRATE ON THE PEAKS.
AMEN.*

THIRD WEEK OF ADVENT

TUESDAY

THE CORE OF THE ESSENTIAL
PASSES MOSTLY THROUGH THE
INESSENTIAL.

ADRIENNE VON SPEYR,
LUMINA AND NEW LUMINA[5]

BUT CAME TO BEAR
WITNESS TO THE LIGHT

Pope John Paul II was once asked by a reporter, "What does the pope do in his free time?" He responded, "I don't understand the question—all my time is free." As a young priest, I desired to be extraordinary like my hero John Paul. But I interpreted it in worldly terms, quietly thinking it connected to the prestige of office and a good reputation. Only when these were taken away could I truly look at the precondition of discipleship: "Whoever of you does not renounce all that he has cannot be my disciple" (Lk 14:33). That was the secret to John Paul's freedom.

Much of the work of renunciation happens in the ordinary, mundane details of daily life. The wheel of time spins us through an unseen, seldom interesting, routine. We resist it and now have the technological prowess to avoid it. But we can embrace it when we locate it in the life of Nazareth, where 90 percent of Christ's life passed as seemingly inessential.

John bears witness to the divine light in its entirety, not simply in extraordinary moments like the baptism and Transfiguration. Christ doesn't offer light—he is light, just as much at home as on itinerancy. When we expand our vision of this, we see it for what it truly is. "He reveals his own light to the world by concealing it in the Father. It is the light of sonship, the light of his particular filial love as it shines toward the Father and toward man."[6] Light and love are united in the freedom of his total sonship.

This inheritance of the Son is the battle of the Christian. "The night is far gone, the day is at hand. Let us then cast off the works of darkness and put on the armor of light" (Rom 13:12). Defenseless we are thrown into the world, not permitted to wield the sword of power (cf. Mt 26:52). All that we are given, all that we need, is the armor of the light. To live in the light is all the protection we need; no harm can be done to those in Christ. With this confidence, we strive to "fight the good fight of faith" (1 Tm 6:12); and in the meantime, we enjoy some free time.

REFLECTION

1. What is the difference between laziness and leisure? How can you add intentional leisure to your daily life?
2. How can you offer even the mundane moments to the Lord?

PRAY

HOLY GOD,
WE ARE NEVER AT REST UNTIL WE REST
IN YOU.
GIVE ME REST THIS ADVENT.
TEACH ME THAT EVEN IN MOMENTS
THAT SEEM INSIGNIFICANT,
YOU ARE WAITING
TO RECEIVE ALL OF ME.
FOR AS ST. TERESA OF AVILA SAYS:
"EVEN WHEN WE ARE IN THE KITCHEN,
OUR LORD MOVES AMONG THE POTS
AND PANS."
TEACH ME TO BE WITH YOU ALWAYS, AS
YOU ARE ALWAYS WITH ME.
AMEN.

THIRD WEEK OF ADVENT

WEDNESDAY

THE DARKNESS HAS TO BECOME
BRIGHTER; BLIND URGE HAD TO
PASS OVER INTO A LOVE THAT
SEES; AND THE CLEVER WILL TO
POSSESS AND DEVELOP HAD TO
BE TRANSFIGURED INTO THE
FOOLISH WISDOM THAT POURS
ITSELF OUT.

HANS URS VON BALTHASAR,
HEART OF THE WORLD[7]

THE TRUE LIGHT THAT ENLIGHTENS EVERY MAN WAS COMING INTO THE WORLD

It was in a stained-glass window in a forgotten side chapel outside of Chicago that I discovered the Mother of God. I knew many things about her, but in that indescribable moment, she became a new and living reality. It was a window into the mystery of the Immaculate Conception, the prevenient grace given to the woman destined to be the *Theotokos*, or "God-bearer."

What John prefigures is now realized in Mary. "It is a shining movement of light to which God can add the grace of being a revelation of the light. Through grace men can show one another God, give one another God, and reveal God to one another."[8] The grace of the Immaculate Conception was given singularly in order that a *fiat* could be made all-encompassing. Mary's "yes" to the Father ushers in salvation. Just as the true light always and forever illuminates Mary's soul, so too is her assent the full revelation of the light.

But for Mary, Christmas is not the end of the story. Her life, co-extensive with her son's, has a trajectory toward the Cross. The luminosity of the *fiat* must shine in the darkness of Calvary if she is to become the New Eve and the true "mother of the living" (Gn 3:20). Just as she stands as the Church at the moment of the Incarnation, so too will she be the Church at the Cross, offering her silent *fiat* on behalf of all creation.

Mary's path from crib to Cross is a trail blazed for all Christians. And as a mother she remains our guide up the mountain that is Christ. Treading this path means becoming a living paradox: death into life, the folly of a new wisdom. By it we are emptied of ego and made translucent—stained glass to bring forth the light.

REFLECTION

1. Have you taken Mary as your own mother? If so, why, and how is that manifested in your life? If not, why not, and how can you beg for the grace to do so?
2. Where is one space in your life where God is asking you to give your *fiat* to him?

_____

_____

_____

_____

_____

_____

_____

_____

_____

_____

PRAY

BLESSED MOTHER,
YOU ARE THE GOD-BEARER, THEOTOKOS,
YOU ARE THE FIRST TABERNACLE.
PREPARE A PLACE IN ME,
LIKE THAT IN YOU,
FOR JESUS CHRIST TO ENTER DURING
THIS COMING CHRISTMAS SEASON.
PREPARE ME FOR THE CRADLE SO THAT
I MAY NOT FAINT AT THE CROSS.
AMEN.

THIRD WEEK OF ADVENT

THURSDAY

IT HAD SEEMED TO STRUGGLE
WITH THE DARKNESS, HAD
SEEMED TO SINK DOWN INTO
THE MIRE,
OVERCOME BY THE CHAOS; BUT
NO ENEMY IS MIGHTIER AND
NO NIGHT MORE NIGHT-FILLED
THAN THE RADIANT DARKNESS
OF LOVE.

HANS URS VON BALTHASAR,
HEART OF THE WORLD[9]

HE WAS IN THE WORLD

The Beatniks used to hang out in a place called My Brother's Bar. It's one of the last great institutions of "old Denver," and it was there on a winter's night that I first heard the story of Odysseus. In Book XII of Homer's *Odyssey*, the protagonist Odysseus is forced to traverse the narrow waters between the Scylla and Charybdis. Scylla is a monstrous female creature that comes out of a cave to attack passing sailors. On the other side lay Charybdis, whose all-consuming thirst creates a whirlpool effect, trapping and shipwrecking those who attempt to pass by. Without facing these impossible circumstances, Odysseus's return to his wife Penelope and homeland of Ithaca are only a passing dream.

The world is filled with such perils. Whether they are the aggressing Scylla or the collapsing Charybdis, both lead to human destruction. It is the great darkness that has set in ever since the originating Fall of man. But as the poet Hopkins says, "There lives the dearest freshness deep down things." We are not Manicheans, who believe the world to be evil. The world is damaged, wounded by sin—but not destroyed. It is to this world that God comes, born of the flesh (Jn 1:1). And it is this that he loves: "for God so loved the world" (Jn 3:16).

"As long as I am in the world, I am the light of the world" (Jn 9:5). The presence of Christ remains in the world and remains precisely as light. It is not his physical body, glorified in the Resurrection and assumed into heaven. It is in his mystical body (the Church) that Christ remains the light of the world. But mere membership in the Church does not necessitate that we are a new creation: "In the new creation the center of gravity is transposed to God. The weight is shifted."[10] This is the great task of conversion, the harrowing path between the Scylla and Charybdis.

REFLECTION

1. How does your experience of suffering change when you remember that nothing can touch you without God's first permitting it?
2. How do you experience the adventure of conversion in your daily life?

PRAY

PRECIOUS JESUS,
YOU ARE ALWAYS WITH ME.
YOU NEVER LEAVE MY SIDE.
MAKE ME MORE AWARE
OF YOUR PRESENCE
AS I JOURNEY THROUGH THIS WORLD
OF TOIL AND SNARE
ON MY WAY HOME TO THE PLACE YOU
HAVE PREPARED FOR ME.
TEACH ME TO LOVE AS YOU LOVE
SO THAT I MAY
PUBLICLY BEAR YOUR IMAGE.
TEACH ME TO BLEED AS YOU BLEED
SO THAT I MAY FULLY REJOICE
AT YOUR BIRTH.
AMEN.

THIRD WEEK OF ADVENT

FRIDAY

LOVE IS AWAKENED BY WHAT IS
BEAUTIFUL, BY WHAT PLEASES
US,
BY WHAT DOES NOT APPEAR
UNWORTHY OF OUR LOVE.

HANS URS VON BALTHASAR,
HEART OF THE WORLD[11]

AND THE WORLD WAS MADE THROUGH HIM

For a fortnight, Caravaggio would paint a masterpiece and then head out on a drunken bender of equal length. But in November of 1600 he beat up the wrong guy—Girolamo Stampa da Montepulciano. This was the beginning of the end. From then on, his life would be punctuated by nights of imprisonment and days of outstanding artistry.

The first Caravaggio I ever saw was in "The Entombment of Christ" in the Pinacoteca of the Vatican Museum. It is utterly massive and totally captivating. It was not the brilliant colors, nor the realistic figures, that caught me; it was his ability to communicate form through *chiaroscuro*, the contrast of light and darkness. This play of light as it radiates in the darkness, also known as *tenebrism*, remains the most lasting impression. Perhaps it was because Caravaggio knew light and darkness in himself.

"Light and darkness, bless the Lord" (Dn 3:72). These words are part of a canticle of praise offered by three young men thrown into a fiery furnace. In them the fires of love burn forth the new life of resurrection. Their ancient prophecy points to the fullness of time, where "the world was made through him" (Jn 1:10) for a second time. From now on, "there is nothing hid, except to be made manifest; nor is anything secret, except to come to light" (Mk 4: 22). But how this is accomplished defies our comprehension. The darkness of sin is destroyed, the light of grace given. But grace imparts a form, one that we continue to reject. "The world refuses to correspond to the new form. It does not want to be what it was intended: it refuses to be the world of the word and refuses to belong to the word."[12] If we acknowledge this in ourselves, the bright light of divine love will appear as darkness. We must bless it and, like Caravaggio, allow our hearts to be painted in *chiaroscuro*.

REFLECTION

1. We cannot know the light if we have not first experienced the darkness. What dark moment or season of your life eventually brought you closer to the Lord?
2. What dark moments or seasons in your life have yet to be resolved? How do you believe God wants to pour graces into these moments?

_____

_____

_____

_____

_____

_____

PRAY

HEALING FATHER,
YOU ARE THE DIVINE PHYSICIAN.
COME INTO THE DARKNESS
OF MY HEART,
AND TRANSFORM IT WITH YOUR
MARVELOUS RAYS.
DO NOT SIMPLY CONTRAST THE
DARKNESS WITHIN ME,
BUT UTTERLY TRANSFORM ME INTO
YOUR LIGHT AND LOVE.
HEAL WITHIN ME WHAT IS BROKEN BY
INJUSTICE AND MALICE.
REMIND ME THAT DARKNESS DOES NOT
HAVE THE FINAL SAY; YOU DO.
AMEN.

THIRD WEEK OF ADVENT

SATURDAY

ALL THAT IS TRANSITORY
IS SHIPWRECKED ON THE
SANDBANKS OF REALITY.

HANS URS VON BALTHASAR,
*YOU CROWN THE YEAR
WITH YOUR GOODNESS*[13]

YET THE WORLD KNEW HIM NOT

Most of my childhood was spent in a hockey locker room, and it was there that I learned to fight. By fight I mean not just physical fighting (which we did) but to take up the spirit of a fighter. If a player hits your goalie after the whistle, then "an eye for an eye, and a tooth for a tooth" (Lv 24:20). It was a school of loyalty, competition, comradery, and most importantly, of justice.

For many years I carried this spirit into the Christian life, even into the priesthood. And it has taken a long time to translate it into the mystery of Christ. Strangely, I now no longer pray for justice. There are still moments of exasperation, seeing an empty penalty box and opponents skating free. But something far greater and more expansive is at work than our petty narratives of betrayal and pain: "In Christ God was reconciling the world to himself" (2 Cor 5:19).

Christ alone offers the expansion of our vision. Only by his atoning sacrifice is there any salvation from the hell of our victim mentality. Original sin is humanity's existential penalty box, and that means we all stand under judgment. "And this is the judgment, that the light has come into the world, and men loved darkness rather than light, because their deeds were evil" (Jn 3:19).

We knew him not. Apart from grace, we do not recognize him, because our center of gravity lies not in God but in ourselves. From that vantage point, we can never know him, know the truth and the reality of his salvific forgiveness. Our work then is to shift the center to Christ, letting the stammering cries of the grasping ego to be silenced in the presence of the living God. It is a work of receptivity, of surrendered measures and expectations. "To receive God means to give oneself to God, even if our gift consists only in offering him our darkness so that his light may shine in it."[14] What I learned in the locker room remains true—life is a fight. Now the task is to understand who and what we are fighting for.

REFLECTION

1. In what small (or big) ways do you forget that you are loved and forgiven by God on a daily basis?
2. What or who is most valuable to you? Is Christ above that thing or person? If not, make him so.

_____

_____

_____

_____

_____

_____

_____

PRAY

SWEET JESUS,
YOU ARE OUR MIGHTY VICTOR.
WE CANNOT WIN A SINGLE FIGHT
WITHOUT YOUR GRACE BEING ALWAYS
WITH US.
REMIND ME TODAY THAT I WILL NEVER
LOOK INTO THE EYES OF ANOTHER
WHO IS NOT FIRST LOVED BY YOU.
HELP ME TO FIGHT FOR THESE SOULS
WHOM YOU SO LOVE,
THAT I MAY, BY YOUR GRACE ALONE,
WIN GREATER TREASURE
FOR YOUR KINGDOM.
AMEN.

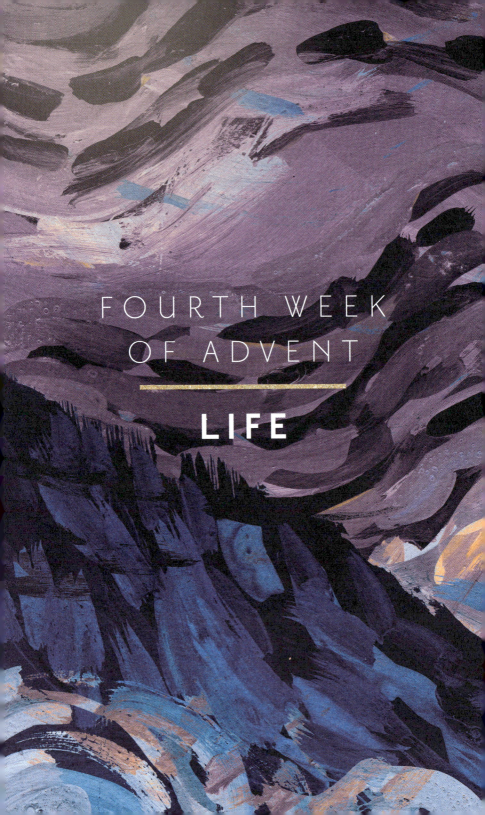

FOURTH WEEK
OF ADVENT

LIFE

FOURTH WEEK OF ADVENT

SUNDAY

ALL THINGS OWE THEMSELVES
TO THIS WORD BUT WHO IT
REALLY IS IN TRUTH IS REVEALED
TO THE WORLD ONLY IF THIS
MOST UNIVERSAL BECOMES A
SINGLE, SPECIFIC, INDIVIDUAL
HUMAN PERSON.

HANS URS VON BALTHASAR,
LIGHT OF THE WORD[1]

HE CAME TO HIS OWN HOME

There was nothing extraordinary about the hermitage other than the silence. Walls of cut cedar envelop a simple room, crafted and directed toward a large bay window facing westward. It sits at the fringe of an aspen grove, peeking out onto a verdant valley near the headwaters of the Colorado River. There one beholds the unnamed mountains upon the continental divide.

A hermitage is a most radical simplification of life. It is a stripping away of all things to the essentials. It is a return to a primordial life, to the epochs of human history that lived quietly in the solitude of creation. But a hermitage is not a place of absence, but of presence. From the Greek *eremos,* "hermitage" means a solitary, desolate place. It was the preferred place of Jesus, the place to which he invites his disciples. "Come away by yourselves to a lonely place (*eremos*), and rest a while" (Mk 6:31).

Jesus makes his home in creation. It is not his original home, which is within the eternal trinitarian life of God. But he nonetheless "came to his own home" (Jn 1:11) in the world. "It is his own because he created it. It is also his own because it was given him by the Father. A strange gift—which does not want to know or hear about him and is in deadly opposition to him."[2] This is symbolized by Jesus's return to his physical hometown in Nazareth, a place of total rejection: "A prophet is not without honor, except in his own country, and among his own kin, and in his own house" (Mk 6:4). The same applies for the home of Christ in the hermitage of our souls. This is a reason we don't want to live at home with him. We would be forced to face our sins and feel his rejection. But it is his chosen place, an indwelling capable of deep union with the Father. Only by doing so can he accomplish his mission: "To give light to those who sit in darkness and in the shadow of death, to guide our feet into the way of peace" (Lk

1:79). So let us set aside all that is of the world and again find the light of Christ in the hermitage of our souls.

REFLECTION

1. St. John Paul II says, "Only in silence does man succeed in hearing . . . the voice of God, which really makes him free." How can you incorporate moments of intentional, attentive silence into your daily life?
2. The pilgrim Christian is called to prayer and resting in Christ's presence by making him a sort of home apart from this earth. What does making Christ your "home" look like for you?
3. How is it possible that, amid the chaos of the world, there can be a quiet oasis within our souls for Christ to dwell? How do we make our souls an oasis?

_____

_____

_____

_____

_____

_____

_____

_____

PRAY

MOTHER MARY,
YOU WERE CHRIST'S FIRST HOME ON
THIS EARTH.
FOR HIM, YOU MADE A SPACE OF
SILENT GROWTH AND LOVE.
TEACH ME TO DO THE SAME
THIS ADVENT.
TEACH ME HOW TO PREPARE A PLACE
WORTHY FOR A KING.
MAKE OF MY SOUL A HERMITAGE FOR
MY LORD.
AMEN.

95

A GOD WHO WAS A MASON AND
A CARPENTER FOR THIRTY YEARS
CAN SURELY MAKE SHORT WORK
OF THE RUINS OF MY SOUL.

HANS URS VON BALTHASAR,
THE GRAIN OF WHEAT[3]

AND HIS OWN PEOPLE
RECEIVED HIM NOT

I was totally disregarded by the hardened workers of the construction site. And rightly so. A priest-theologian walks onto the scene, charged with overseeing the construction of a new seminary gym. Eventually I found a hardhat and spoke to the foreman. The excavation was finished, and the foundation work had begun. To build a gym with structural integrity requires seventy-eight caissons—cement cylinders reaching deep below the structure, grounding it in the invisible bedrock below.

Sometimes human relationships are built without caissons. The ground shifts, the building moves, and friendships suddenly collapse. This experience of unreconciled relationships may be the most devastating thing in human life. It is nothing short of cruciform powerlessness. But to live unreconciled is not the same as to live in unforgiveness. The latter is an absolute mandate of the Gospel. We can always forgive, but sometimes we cannot reconcile. Now we understand his paradoxical words: "Love your enemies" (Mt 5:44).

Our foundations in Christ lay much deeper than our own consent to God. We are "his own" (Jn 1:11) not because of something we did but because of his personal and utterly intentional election of us. "You did not choose me, but I chose you and appointed you that you should go and bear fruit and that your fruit should abide" (Jn 15:16). Our election arises out of the unilateral reconciliation accomplished by Jesus on the Cross. This is the miracle: We continually reject Christ, sabotage our relationship through sin—and yet the building stands. This foundational mystery is the hidden bedrock of our lives.

"Therefore be careful lest the light in you be darkness" (Lk 11:35). There remains a promethean temptation to "fix" the unreconciled aspects of our lives. We attempt this because we want to feel "okay." But our wounded logic cannot ascertain light and distinguish it from darkness. From the ruins, we attempt to plunge back into the ground, to reinstall and fortify buildings that have already been lost. In doing so, we eclipse the possibility of Christological healing, of the new life promised us in Christ. "The important thing is to be possessed by the Lord, and that happened while we were still sinners. For he chose us, not we him."[4] Sometimes miracles happen, and reconciliation is restored. Other times we receive nothing other than the mystery of the Cross, laid bare before us. Regardless, our task is to live in the construction site, lay the caissons, and entrust all workmanship to the carpenter of Nazareth.

REFLECTION

1. What does a strong relationship built on Christ's love look like to you?
2. Have you allowed broken relationships in your past to be healed by Christ? If not, how does one go about doing so, and why should they?
3. You are only able to love because Christ first loved you. How should you treat your relationships with others while keeping this in mind?

PRAY

FATHER IN HEAVEN,
YOU ARE THE CREATOR AND LOVER
MOST HIGH.
DO NOT LET ME FORGET THE LOVE
YOU HAVE FOR ME.
ALLOW THIS LOVE TO SHAPE THE
RELATIONSHIPS WITH
THOSE AROUND ME.
FOR THOSE BROKEN RELATIONSHIPS IN
MY PAST, BE MY HEALING.
FOR MOMENTS OF RECONCILIATION
AND PEACE, BE MY FORGIVENESS.
. BE THE CARPENTER OF
THE LOVE I GIVE.
AMEN.

FOURTH WEEK OF ADVENT

TUESDAY

THE MORE LOVE ONE RECEIVES,
THE POORER ONE IS. THE MORE
LOVE ONE GIVES AWAY, THE
RICHER ONE BECOMES. WEALTH
FINALLY BECOMES LIMITLESS,
IN FACT, ONLY WHEN IT HAS
BECOME NAKED POVERTY.

ADRIENNE VON SPEYR,
LUMINA AND NEW LUMINA[5]

BUT TO ALL WHO RECEIVED HIM

I was standing in a Barnes & Noble, looking at a section entitled "Religion and Spirituality." Newly converted to the faith, I sought to "be conformed to this world" no longer but to be "transformed by the renewal of your mind" (Rom 12:2). But from the look of it, all I could see was Christianity transformed into the world. Beneath tomes of sophisticated critique and transcendental meditation, I found a small book by a man named Francis. I opened it to a prayer called *The Instrument of Peace* and read this line: "It is in giving that we receive."

The ocean of love is found on the shores of giving and receiving. And their relationship is a paradox. At times it seems that giving is better; as we hear in the Acts of the Apostles, "it is more blessed to give than to receive" (Acts 20:35). But at other times, greatness in the Christian life is defined as receptivity, specifically of the childlike (cf. Mk 9:37). What then is their relationship? Everything hinges first on Christ's revelation of the inner trinitarian life and then upon how we in creation stand in relation to it. This is the spiritual revolution of Jesus.

"True religion consists in neither trying to become God (mysticism) nor persisting in creaturely distance from God (Judaism, Islam), rather, true religion is to attain supreme union with God precisely on the basis of the lasting distinction between Creator and creature."[6] Everything hinges on the Incarnation—that is, the descending of the Creator God into creation in the form of man. We cannot know God apart from this descent, which St. Paul describes as "kenotic," or self-emptying (cf. Phil 2:6). When God's love gives and is emptied, we—and the entire world—are received. Now "all those who received him" know the truth of love (Jn 1:12). The call is to fight the instinct of self-preservation and trust the poor man from Assisi. "It is in giving that we receive."

REFLECTION

1. In what ways have you made your heart poor—lacking the riches of heaven?
2. What aversions do you have toward poverty (physical or spiritual)? How are those aversions preventing you from trusting in the Lord's provision?
3. Consider the poverty of the infant of Jesus. How is the Lord calling you to imitate him this Advent and into the Christmas season?

PRAY

MOST IMPOVERISHED JESUS,
DO NOT LET ME IGNORE YOU, OH
BEGGAR OF LOVE.
DRAW ME CLOSE TO YOU
IN ALL YOUR HUMILITY
SO THAT I MAY COME TO SEE YOU
IN YOUR FULL SPLENDOR.
MAY I BE ONE WHO RECEIVES YOU
THIS SEASON,
SO THAT I MAY IMITATE YOUR
CHILDLIKE POVERTY
AND THAT I MAY BECOME FAMILIAR
WITH THE EMBRACE OF THE FATHER.
AMEN.

THOSE WHO WORK IN THE LIGHT
DO NOT NEED TO DRAG THEIR
WORD INTO THE SPOTLIGHT.

ADRIENNE VON SPEYR,
LUMINA AND NEW LUMINA[7]

WHO BELIEVED IN HIS NAME

The beginning of my acting career was as Bob Cratchit in a sixth-grade production of *A Christmas Carol*. It was also the end of my career (if that says anything about my talent as a thespian). But regardless of our capacity, all human beings carry an innate sense of the dramatic. We wake each morning with the expectant hope that we will live out our call to be the protagonist of our existence. And it is each night that we retire, defeated and frustrated, by those other protagonists sharing the stage.

It is then to Christ that we must look to resolve the theodramatic tension of our lives. And he does so in the most peculiar of manners—by self-denial and the hiddenness of faith. St. Paul reminds us: "You have died and your life is hidden with Christ in God" (Col 3:3). Those who take on the name of Christ have no place in the spotlight, no regard for prominence (even on the stage of the Church). Like Odysseus at the mast, we must resist the siren call of accolades, good reputation, and self-importance. And the deepest surrender is our self-perfected plan of holiness. For "to strive for one's own perfection is a bourgeois ideal."[8]

The little way of Jesus is followed along the path of Marian childlikeness. "The heart, man's center, where soul and body are one, must decide to become a womb for God's seed. Here the heart, the most secret and yet most vulnerable, the most central and yet most exposed part of man, has the power to open or close itself."[9] Perhaps the hardest thing in life is to keep our hearts open to God. Those "who believed in his name" (Jn 1:14)—namely, the saints—have done so, abiding in the realm of perfect, disinterested freedom. They alone know the secret of drama, described by Hopkins in his poem "As Kingfishers Catch Fire": "Christ plays in ten thousand places, / Lovely in limbs, and lovely in eyes not his / To the Father through the features of men's faces."

REFLECTION

1. In what ways do you find yourself longing for the "spotlight" in your spiritual life?
2. What is one practical way you can seek humility in this area?
3. What is one practical way you can turn the spotlight onto Christ today (even in the small, mundane things)?

PRAY

HOLY JESUS,
IT IS YOUR NAME I FIGHT FOR,
NOT MY OWN.
LET ALL I DO, ALL I SAY, ALL I LONG
FOR, BE IN PRAISE OF YOUR MOST
HOLY NAME, JESUS.
NOT TO US, OH LORD, NOT TO US,
BUT TO YOUR NAME
BE THE GLORY (PS 115:1).
NOT IN THE LIGHT OF FAME DO I WANT
TO BASK,
BUT IN THE LIGHT OF YOUR MOST
HOLY WILL.
GIVE ME NOT POPULARITY, BUT ONLY
YOUR LOVE AND YOUR GRACE.
YOU ARE ENOUGH FOR ME.
AMEN.

FOURTH WEEK OF ADVENT

THURSDAY

IN ORDER FOR GOD'S LIGHT
TRULY TO SHINE IN THE
DARKNESS, THE DARKNESS MUST,
AS IT WERE,
RECEIVE IT INTO ITSELF, WRAP
ITSELF AROUND IT.

HANS URS VON BALTHASAR,
YOU HAVE WORDS OF ETERNAL LIFE[10]

HE GAVE POWER TO
BECOME CHILDREN OF GOD

Where we came from matters. My father is a West Point trained Army Ranger; my mother, a sorority girl from northern Minnesota. This makes for a unique personality, to say the least. Everyone has their endowment, a lineage traced back to the original parents. Each strand of DNA has been shaped by culture and times, by decisions made or not made. Our ancestry is impossibly complex, and yet we can't understand ourselves without it. Though our actions, and not our past, are what make our lives what they become, there is no self-creation. We are members of a family that stretches to the first days of human history.

The Christian life is a birth. It is not wholly supernatural but builds upon our nature. It arises out of reception and takes the form of a gift. There is no knowledge of Christ, no discipleship upon his path, without this rebirth and new life. But how? Nicodemus first poses this question in the darkness of night. And Our Lord responds: "Truly, truly, I say to you, unless one is born anew, he cannot see the kingdom of God" (Jn 3:3). This childhood is a sharing in the light, at once a patrimony and a task. "While you have the light, believe in the light, that you may become sons of light" (Jn 12:36).

The essence of Christianity is then childhood in the light. As much as they may contribute, no therapy or technology can bring us into the light of Christ. The gift of a new childhood transcends our notions not just of light and darkness but of time and eternity as well. "As we begin to be children of God the fact we had thought so clear and definite within us into eternal life, which is always in the beginning, with God, and overflows eternally."[11] Forty years ago, a ranger and a sorority girl brought a child to the baptismal font. There he was filled with light. Now his one task is faith, that he become a son of the light.

REFLECTION

1. When you remember that you are a child of God, and that you exist only because God wants you to, how does your world-view change?
2. How do you play your role of "child of the light" in your life?

PRAY

JESUS, SON OF GOD,
YOU ARE THE ONE WHO BRINGS ALL
SOULS FROM DARKNESS
INTO YOUR LIGHT.
INFUSE IN ME AN UNDERSTANDING OF
MY IDENTITY IN YOU.
YOU HAVE NOT LEFT ME ORPHAN,
AND YOU NEVER WILL.
HELP ME TO LIVE AS ONE WHO HAS
BEEN CLAIMED BY LOVE HIMSELF.
AMEN.

FOURTH WEEK OF ADVENT

FRIDAY

THE CHURCH ON EARTH IS THIS
OPENING, THIS OPENNESS OF
GOD TO THE WORLD;
SHE IS THE PLACE WHERE THIS
OPENING TAKES PLACE AND
BECOMES A KNOWN REALITY.

HANS URS VON BALTHASAR,
YOU CROWN THE YEAR
WITH YOUR GOODNESS[12]

WHO WERE BORN, NOT OF BLOOD NOR OF THE WILL OF THE FLESH

A priest friend of mine tells a story. It is Christmas Day, and he is watching his nephews play with newly opened toys. A fight ensues, their mom intervenes, and a powerful theological idea is communicated. Taking away the toy, she says to them, "Remember, neither of you actually own anything." Every family life is the first ambit, daresay battlefield, over the goods of life. The chilling distinction of "mine and thine" plays out in our fallen nature, and it is the task of parents to educate little ones into the reality of gift and dispossession.

As the prologue of John concludes, the meaning of rebirth is clarified (cf. Jn 1:13). It is not from blood—that is, from sex, race, kin, or inheritance. It is neither the will of the flesh, meaning from the deep human strata of instinct and desire. Lastly, it is not from the will of man—that is, from a self-perfecting pattern of holiness. To be born of God is a total mystery, utterly unknowable. "The birth is accomplished in such absolute secrecy that to the majority of men it remains completely hidden. They have grace without knowing how they received it. They are children of God without knowing what it means."[13] This is the Church in her pure essence, the opening of man to God.

To be born *of* God requires the daily task of letting things remain *from* God. This is the great challenge of living in the light. Divine charity is the manifestation of the light, and the condition upon which things remain from God. "He who says he is in the light and hates his brother is in the darkness still. He who loves his brother abides in the light, and in it there is no cause for stumbling" (1 Jn 2:9–10). Little people understand the tragedy and triumph implied in every loss and gain. We adults think ourselves better when in fact we are far more deceived. For we, too, don't actually own anything.

1. What is one practical way that you can remind yourself that God is in control at all times?
2. How do you remind yourself that you don't actually own anything?
3. How does your life become more peaceful, more free, when you acknowledge regularly that you are taken care of by God in every moment?

PRAY

HEAVENLY FATHER,
YOU ARE ALL POWERFUL
AND ALL KNOWING.
TAKE CONTROL OF MY LIFE, MY
POSSESSIONS, MY ANXIETIES,
AND REDEEM THEM SO THAT THEY
BECOME ENTIRELY YOURS.
I CANNOT BE FULLY MYSELF IF I AM
NOT FULLY YOURS.
RELEASE ME FROM ATTACHMENTS THAT
WEIGH ME DOWN;
SET ME FREE FROM BURDENS OF WHICH
YOU DO NOT APPROVE.
MAY ALL THIS BE DONE FOR GREATER
GLORY OF YOUR NAME.
AMEN.

FOURTH WEEK OF ADVENT

CHRISTMAS EVE

GOD IS NOT IN A HURRY.

HANS URS VON BALTHASAR,
LIGHT OF THE WORD[14]

NOR OF THE WILL OF MAN, BUT OF GOD

I had a shirt in high school that read, "There is no need to worry or be in a hurry." A lyric from the band String Cheese Incident, I imagine I wore it as a way of convincing myself it were true. But there are of course many reasons to worry or be in a hurry. In the end, I only wore the slogan like a shirt; it never became a part of me.

Then the day comes when we confront the mystery of the child Jesus in the arms of his mother. The setting of Bethlehem effects a kind of stillness that envelops the escalating pace of our frenetic world. Mary knew haste (cf. Lk 1:39) but never hurry. Why? Because she understood a great truth only fully revealed at the Cross: namely, that through the gift of Christ's atoning sacrifice, time is refashioned. "Christmas is no celebration of niceness, rather it celebrates the powerlessness of God's love, which can overpower only by means of death."[15] Powerlessness is the true form of Christian repose. "Be still and know that I am God" (Ps 46:10).

In these last hours before the birth of Christ, we turn to the place where he abides—the womb of his mother. "If we look at Mary, the towering central point between Israel and the Church, our gaze rests on something utterly concrete; we see our sister, who succeeded in doing for us what, in virtue of her example, we must attempt to emulate, namely, to allow God's Word to dwell in us bodily."[16] The most important word on Mary in the New Testament appears as insignificant: "When the time had fully come, God sent forth his Son, born of woman" (Gal 4:4). Mary inhabits time differently because she gives birth to "the fullness of time" (Eph 1:10). And this fullness extends her motherhood eternally, to all people, places, and times. Just as God was born of a woman two thousand years ago, every birth of God through baptism and faith in the soul occurs in and through the mother-hood of God. She is truly our mother, the mother of the Church. And she is in no hurry.

REFLECTION

1. Set aside a moment of silent prayer in your day today (maybe five, ten, or fifteen minutes). What happens in your heart?
2. Is your life one of hurry or one of haste? Though you may not be able to change your busy schedule, what is one way you can incorporate a sense of patience into it?

PRAY

MOTHER MARY,
TEACH ME TO LIVE LIKE YOU.
TEACH ME TO DO THE WILL
OF YOUR SON,
NOT WITH RUSHING AND ANXIETY,
BUT WITH PATIENCE
AND DIVINE EFFICIENCY.
AMEN.

119

FOURTH WEEK OF ADVENT

CHRISTMAS DAY

CHRISTMAS IS NOT AN EVENT
WITHIN HISTORY BUT IS RATHER
THE INVASION OF TIME BY
ETERNITY.

HANS URS VON BALTHASAR,
LIGHT OF THE WORD[17]

AND THE WORD BECAME FLESH AND DWELT AMONG US, FULL OF GRACE AND TRUTH

Christmas morning began at an ungoldly hour. My parents, disheveled and uncaffeinated, worked to corral our enthusiasm and bring some semblance of order to the opening of presents. Having ripped through them like savages, we now stood before our bounty like conquerors of a new land. And then we found it: a last, tiny present hidden in the recesses of the tree. We opened it to find a note: "Look under the sink." Running to the sink, we found another note: "Look under your pillow." The notes continued throughout the house as our adventure accelerated. By the time we reached the end of the journey in the basement, we could not believe our eyes: a fully setup ping-pong table—the greatest gift we would ever receive.

You may be asking yourself if this were in fact the greatest of gifts. It may not be, and in fact, it very likely wasn't. But decades later it is impressed in my memory precisely because of the way the gift was disclosed. It was a stroke of a paternal genius, making the ordinary seem extraordinary through the rhythm of hiddenness and disclosure.

The season of Advent is the chase throughout the house, picking up on hints and guesses led by an omnibenevolent Father. It concludes today, the Feast of Christmas, with the unexpected and greatest of gifts. Shepherds and Magi were led in the same way to the crib. And if we are to fight off the bored expectancy of human life, we must embrace again today the mystery of the truly unexpected. "The Word became flesh and dwelt among us" (Jn 1:14). No truer or greater words have ever been spoken. This is the event that decides all of history, the knife that cuts through every human heart. Either God is Word and made incarnate, or we are left with a wordless and disincarnated life. The choice is God or nothing, and he hinges everything on the birth of his Son. It is from within this mystery that the transformation of the world is born. "The spiritual Word became flesh so that our flesh might become spiritual. Because the Son became as we are, we can become as he is: children of God."[18]

As the life of St. John is quietly ending on the Island of Patmos, he is given a last glimpse into heaven. "And I heard a loud voice from the throne saying, 'Behold, the dwelling of God is with men. He will dwell with them, and they shall be his people, and God himself will be with them'" (Rv 21:3). This is the mystery of Christmas in eschatological fulfillment. It is the Incarnate Word having returned to the Father, now with all of creation in him. "And night shall be no more; they need no light of lamp or sun, for the Lord God will be their light, and they shall reign for ever and ever" (Rv 22:5). Christmas is already the end of history and the beginning of eternity. And it is all light.

REFLECTION

1. It is often not the gifts God gives that cause us to love him but the way he gives them. How has God given you gifts in the past?

2. God will never stop giving us his graces as long as we are open to receiving them. What is one practical way you can make yourself open to receiving God's gifts throughout the coming new year?

3. During Advent, how has God spoken to your heart in a new way? How will you allow this new light to guide you closer to the Lord?

_____

_____

PRAY

JESUS,
THANK YOU FOR THE ADVENT SEASON,
WHICH BRINGS ME EVER READY FOR
YOUR BIRTH.
THANK YOU FOR YOUR WONDROUS
HUMILITY IN COMING TO ME WHEN I
REFUSED TO COME TO YOU.
COME INTO EVERY ASPECT OF MY LIFE
THIS DAY.
JESUS, COME BE MY HOPE.
SHOW ME THE LIGHT OF YOUR
INCARNATION BROUGHT FORTH BY
HEAVENLY LOVE.
JESUS, COME BE MY PEACE.
LET ME BECOME FULLY AGLOW WITH
YOUR RADIANCE.
JESUS, COME BE MY JOY.
FILL ME CONSTANTLY WITH YOUR
GRACE AND TRUTH.
JESUS, COME BE MY LOVE.
JESUS, COME BE MY LIGHT.
AMEN.

NOTES

EPIGRAPH

Hans Urs von Balthasar, *You Crown the Year with Your Goodness: Sermons Throughout the Liturgical Year* (San Francisco: Ignatius Press, 1998), 255.

FIRST WEEK OF ADVENT: WORD

1. Adrienne von Speyr, *The Word: A Meditation on the Prologue to St. John's Gospel*, trans. Alexander Dru (David McKay Company, 1953), 17.

2. Von Speyr, *The Word*, 14.

3. Hans Urs von Balthasar, *The Grain of Wheat: Aphorisms* (San Francisco: Ignatius Press, 1995), 84.

4. Von Speyr, *The Word*, 15.

5. Von Balthasar, *The Grain of Wheat*, 12.

6. Von Speyr, *The Word*, 18.

7. Adrienne von Speyr, *Lumina and New Lumina* (San Francisco: Ignatius Press, 2008), 107.

8. Von Speyr, *The Word*, 29.

9. Von Balthasar, *The Grain of Wheat*, 12.

10. Von Speyr, *The Word*, 26.

11. Hans Urs von Balthasar, *You Have Words of Eternal Life: Scripture Meditations* (San Francisco: Ignatius Press, 1991), 89.

12. Von Speyr, *The Word*, 30.

13. Von Speyr, *Lumina*, 19.

14. Von Speyr, *The Word*, 39.

SECOND WEEK OF ADVENT: LIGHT

1. Hans Urs von Balthasar, *Heart of the World* (San Francisco: Ignatius Press, 1980), 165.

2. Von Speyr, *The Word*, 45–46.

3. Von Speyr, *Lumina,* 46.

4. Von Speyr, *The Word*, 50.

5. Von Balthasar, *Heart of the World*, 59.

6. Von Speyr, *The Word*, 53.

7. Von Speyr, *Lumina,* 107.

8. Von Speyr, *The Word*, 65.

9. Von Balthasar, *You Crown the Year,* 205.

10. Von Speyr, *The Word*, 66.

11. Von Balthasar, *You Crown the Year,* 56.

12. Von Speyr, *The Word*, 70.

13. Von Balthasar, *You Have Words of Eternal Life*, 174.

14. Von Speyr, *The Word*, 78.

THIRD WEEK OF ADVENT: FAITH

1. Von Balthasar, *You Crown the Year,* 244.

2. Von Speyr, *The Word*, 68.

3. Hans Urs von Balthasar, *Light of the Word: Brief Reflections on the Sunday Readings* (San Francisco: Ignatius Press, 1993), 153.

4. Von Speyr, *The Word*, 72.

5. Von Speyr, *Lumina,* 31.

6. Von Speyr, *The Word*, 74.

7. Von Balthasar, *Heart of the World*, 40.

8. Von Speyr, *The Word*, 76.

9. Von Balthasar, *Heart of the World*, 72.

10. Von Speyr, *The Word*, 107.

11. Von Balthasar, *Heart of the World*, 64-65.

12. Von Speyr, *The Word*, 106–7.

13. Von Balthasar, *You Crown the Year,* 247.

14. Von Speyr, *The Word*, 109.

FOURTH WEEK OF ADVENT: LIFE

1. Von Balthasar, *Light of the Word*, 33.
2. Von Speyr, *The Word*, 110.
3. Von Balthasar, *The Grain of Wheat*, 50.
4. Von Speyr, *The Word*, 113.
5. Von Speyr, *Lumina*, 41.
6. Von Balthasar, *Light of the Word*, 34.
7. Von Speyr, *Lumina*, 74.
8. Von Balthasar, *The Grain of Wheat*, 105.
9. Von Balthasar, *You Crown the Year*, 194.
10. Von Balthasar, *You Have Words of Eternal Life*, 215.
11. Von Speyr, *The Word*, 118.
12. Von Balthasar, *You Crown the Year*, 140.
13. Von Balthasar, *Light of the Word*, 19.
14. Von Balthasar, *Light of the Word*, 258.
15. Von Balthasar, *Your Crown the Year*, 191.
16. Von Speyr, *The Word*, 127–28.
17. Von Balthasar, *Light of the Word*, 26.
18. Von Speyr, *The Word*, 135.

FR. JOHN NEPIL is vice rector and assistant professor at St. John Vianney Theological Seminary in Denver, Colorado, and cohost of the *Catholic Stuff You Should Know* podcast.

He earned a doctor of sacred theology degree in dogmatic theology from the Pontifical University of the Holy Cross in Rome, Italy.

Nepil is an avid hiker who started preaching in the mountains as a college chaplain in Boulder, Colorado. Since becoming a priest, he has celebrated Mass on the summit of every 14,000-foot mountain in the state.

Website: catholicstuffpodcast.com
Instagram: @catholicstuffpodcast
Facebook: @CatholicStuffPodcast

FREE *Illuminate* Companion Resources and Videos Available

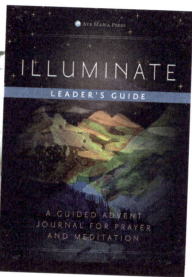

Enhance your Advent experience with these **FREE resources**.
Perfect for **individual use**, **parishes**, **small groups**, and **classroom settings**.

- weekly companion videos with Fr. John Nepil
- *Illuminate Leader's Guide*
- pulpit and bulletin announcements
- downloadable flyers, posters, and digital graphics
- and more!

Scan here to access the free resources and videos or visit
avemariapress.com/pages/illuminate-resources.